LOVE

YOURSELF

Edward Richardson, M.M.

LIGUORI
PUBLICATIONS

One Liguori Drive
Liguori, MO 63057-9999
(314) 464-2500

Imprimi Potest:
Edmund T. Langton, C.SS.R.
Provincial, St. Louis Province
The Redemptorists

Imprimatur:
+ George J. Gottwald
Vicar General, Archdiocese of St. Louis

Liguori Publications

Printed in U.S.A.

Table of Contents

LOVE YOURSELF

Rev. Edward Richardson, M. M.

INTRODUCTION

As I begin to write the final draft of this booklet on the feast of the most holy Trinity, it is a quiet night in the village of Green Mountain in South Korea. I feel a burning desire to communicate to others what I believe to be a treasury of insights that flow from a study of Christ's words, "Love your neighbor as yourself." Although these words of Our Lord are part of the new Law of Love, the phrase "as yourself" is one of the least discussed and least explained elements in spiritual books. And yet, as Our Lord indicates, loving one's self is a foundation, a starting point of the spiritual life.

In discussing this idea with others, I have expressed it in many ways:

"We have an obligation to love ourselves."

"We can't love others if we don't love ourselves."

"We are lovable."

"We commit all kinds of sins because we don't love ourselves."

"Trouble is that we don't love ourselves enough."

"The way to overcome faults and sins is to start loving one's self."

"Sins, faults, neuroses are symptoms of something more basic — a lack of self-love."

The reactions of many people to these statements have frequently been that of surprise, disbelief, and often rather animated disagreement. These ideas seem to clash with some traditional views regarding humility, and man's so-called "corrupt" human nature. Many people think of self-love only in terms of pride. One will say, "What do you mean? My trouble is that I love myself too much!" Another will say, "How can I love myself? I'm rotten, corrupt, good-for-nothing!" However, there is no need to apologize for or to water down Our Lord's words. He meant what He said. "Love your neighbor as yourself." If self-love means pride to some, then it is not the love to which Christ referred. Nevertheless, the notion of loving self is mysterious and paradoxical and needs much explanation.

Recent advances in psychology, especially those made by such men as Carl Rogers and Charles Curran, have given insight into man's nature. With the aid of psychologists, theologians are discovering how and to what extent man is created in the image and likeness of God. From a case-history study of interpersonal relationships much insight has been gained into the nature of love, man's need for it, the effect it has on his personality and moral life, the mutual effects it has on people, its healing quality, and its role in a person's growth into maturity.

That grace permeates and elevates nature is a basic doctrine of the spiritual life. Hence, the more we know about human nature, the better we can understand the operations of grace. The more we learn about ourselves and each other as persons, the better we know Christ. The more we know about man's interpersonal relationships, the better we can understand the Trinity; for the Trinity is a community of persons. And, most importantly, the more deeply we are able to understand human love, the more profoundly we are able to understand divine grace, and

God himself. Why? Because "God is love." Because God's grace is love. Because receiving grace is receiving a share of God's life, and the inner life of the Trinity itself is love.

"The Charity of God is poured forth in our hearts by the Holy Spirit, who is given to us" (Romans 5:5).

Another basic doctrine of the spiritual life is that of spiritual childhood: "Unless you turn and become as little children, you shall not enter the kingdom of heaven" (Matt. 18:1). These words have too often been misinterpreted to mean: "Lower yourself, debase yourself." Think of yourself as nothingness. Don't love yourself." But that is not what Our Lord meant. I hope to show clearly that becoming a child again does not involve underselling ourselves by saying that we are worthless nobodies. It involves something much more positive and beautiful.

I feel convinced that Carl Rogers with his principles derived from client-centered therapy and Charles Curran with similar principles derived from non-directive counseling have provided the basis for deep insight into what it means to "turn and become a child."

It is for two very appropriate reasons that I begin this work on the feast of the most holy Trinity. First, since this is to be a study of interpersonal relationships, there can be no better starting point than the relationships of love that exist between the three persons of the blessed Trinity. More and more, the human capacity to love and be loved is seen by dogmatic theologians to be the stamp of God's image and likeness, since God is love. Theologians have been rethinking their science in more personal and dynamic terms; and there is every reason to believe that from insights into human nature we can arrive at a more profound knowledge of God, and of grace which is a relationship of love that exists between God and man.

Secondly, it was on the feast of the blessed Trinity some 70 years ago that St. Therese, the Little Flower, wrote her "Act of Offering to the Merciful Love of God." This offering is the crowning glory of her little way of spiritual childhood. Her Little Way needs no proof or apologies, for it is the way of the Gospels; but I hope to show that beneath the simplicity of "turning and becoming a child," there lies a profound truth both in psychology and theology.

Edward Richardson, M. M.

CHAPTER I
UNCONDITIONAL LOVE

How does a person begin to love himself or to hate himself? The answer goes back to his childhood. When a child is born, he is good, beautiful, valuable, lovable, a precious diamond.

But at the time of birth, the little baby knows nothing about himself. That is, he does not know whether he is good or bad, lovable or detestable, whether he is of value or worthless. Moreover, in relation to other people, he doesn't know whether he is better or worse, superior or inferior. He does not have a knowledge of his dignity or lack of it. How then does he come to know himself, evaluate himself, and form a self-concept? How does he find his own identity? How does he get to know whether he has worth or not?

It is through interpersonal relationships that he gets to know and love or hate himself. His first contact with people will be his parents. They ordinarily will be the prime influence in his quest for self-identity, in his formation of a self-concept. There are other influences, other variables: brothers, sisters, aunts, friends, grandparents, the TV set, pastors, and all the people he encounters; but for the sake of simplicity, I'll consider just the role of parents in personality formation.

PARENTAL LOVE
When an infant is loved as he is in himself, prized, well taken care of by his parents; when his mother hugs

him, smiles, makes him giggle, gets up at night when he cries, changes his diapers, nurses him when he desires, the child feels secure, happy, and feels accepted and wanted. You can see it in his eyes. On the contrary, when a mother is affectionless, doesn't want to be bothered getting up, when her reaction to the child is frequently one of irritation, displeasure, anger, then the child feels insecure — as if saying to himself: "Do I cause mom to be unhappy? Am I bad? Does she hate me? Am I detestable? Do I cause such a reaction in mom?" Just what a child would say to himself in such an atmosphere could never be proven; but in the eyes of some babies, we can see doubt, anxiety, a fear of people, insecurity.

A few years later when this child begins to talk he thereby enters into a deeper interpersonal relationship with others through vocal communication. At this time, mother and father make frequent conversation with him. Mother will say "Joe, I love you." Father might say, "Joe, you are a good boy." These are simple expressions of love and appreciation, which if sincere and genuine and repeated often enough without conditions and strings attached lead Joe to feel and say, "I am good and lovable; I am worth something."

"IF" LOVE

But when mother or father says, "Joe, if you don't stop pulling baby sister's ears, I won't love you . . . " "You are no good if you make finger prints on the wall" . . . . "Why can't you be like your brother?" . . . "If you want dad to really love you, get an A on your report card" . . . "Joe, you are so cute I just can't help loving you" . . . "I'd love you a lot more if you'd work hard and be more helpful around the house" . . . "If you are

naughty I won't love you" ... "If you don't quit being bad, God too will stop loving you," they are placing conditions on their love for him. They are conveying to him the idea that he is good, worthwhile, loved and lovable only if ... if ... if ... if he does something, avoids something, becomes something, possesses something (e.g. cuteness), or achieves something. He is not able to feel lovable as he is in himself and for his own sake; instead he is led to feel that he must first satisfy some demand, avoid something, or do something, or achieve some goal.

Parents without ever using the word "if" can convey this idea by their attitudes, by turning their love on and off according as the child meets or fails to meet their demands or conditions, by showing favoritism, by using love as a reward, by turning off love as a punishment, by being overly strict, by holding grudges and constantly reminding a child of past failings, and by threatening to stop loving a child if he does such and such.

"SWEET DOMINATION"

Another form of conditional love perhaps more harmful than the forcefully dominating and demanding type (because of its deceptiveness) is what we might call "sweet domination." In this case, one or both parents love Joe because they need him, because they are starving for love, perhaps due to their own emotional insecurity. The child is loved to death almost literally. In a sweet and winning way, the parent does everything to win the child's love by keeping him dependent, to the extent that he dies as a person, or does not even become a person. Here Joe is not loved for his own sake, but because they need him simply as a means to satisfy their excessive craving to love and be loved. It is deceptive because such a child can go on all through life insisting that he was always loved by his parents while at the same time unconsciously rebelling and feeling unloved.

It might be that Joe is loved as a fulfillment of mom or dad, or as a status symbol, or as someone to boast about, or as support for their old age. Whatever the shape or form it takes, such a love is not unconditional, and somehow Joe gets to feel it. When one's parents are cold, unaccepting, or quarrelsome; when they fail to show understanding or approval; or when one lives in a rigid home in which the children are sternly regimented because the parents want peace, quiet, neatness, and order, it is difficult for a child to feel loved.

A DIAMOND

As was mentioned previously, a child at birth does not know what he is. He cannot know his identity — whether he is good or bad, lovable or detestable, worth something or worthless. But we know from philosophy, the empirical sciences, and religion that a child as a human person is a marvelous, good, and beautiful creature. Every single person has a soul that is immortal, indivisible, absolutely simple and imperishable. He has an intellect, free will, uniqueness, the power to love, creativity. Every single person is worth more than the whole material universe, with all its treasures, the sun, the moon, the stars. And more wonderful yet, he is created in the image and likeness of God. Christ by His incarnation gave him dignity, by His blood redeemed him, and by His resurrection promised him future glory. Joe, in truth, is a precious, sparkling diamond — good, of great worth, loved and made lovable by God himself.

But when Joe looks at himself, does he see a diamond? As an infant and as a young child he is not a philosopher, nor a psychologist, nor a theologian. And so, what he sees in himself will result mainly from the attitudes and reactions of people toward him, especially his parents. It is through the reflection of himself in the mirror of other people's reactions and attitudes toward him that he will see, judge, evaluate and thereby come to love or hate himself.

Suppose that the demands made on Joe and the conditions he must fulfill in order to feel loved are one or more of the following: perfection, hard work, honor grades, being like his father or brother, puritanical chastity, good manners and social grace, conformity to a European cultural pattern, piety, becoming a doctor, glorifying the family name, or any other of an endless variety of possible conditions. Suppose further that because of the unreasonableness of the demands or because of his own limitations he cannot fulfill these conditions apparently or really imposed by his parents for being loved and lovable. When this happens, Joe begins to feel disliked and dislikable, worthless and bad, inferior to others, good-for-nothing, and rejected. He feels he is not loved and as a result experiences a starving for love. What then does he see when he looks at himself? Joe does not see the sparkling beautiful diamond that he is. He does not see a *person*. He begins to see himself as a smudged, dark, unlovable and unloved, worthless creature. He might describe himself in any number of ways: "I'm a slob." "I'm no damned good!" "I wish I could be like . . . . " "I can't do anything right." Let's call it a negative self-regard or self-hatred. Or rather let's say simply that Joe does not love himself enough.

CHAPTER II
DEFENSE MECHANISMS

The human heart cannot long endure a condition of not being loved. A continuous experience of feeling unloved – and hence not being capable of loving oneself – causes anxiety, conflict, frustration and fear. Why? Because God put in us an unquenchable desire to love and to be loved. Feeling unloved takes away joy, peace, and balance. It brings on anxiety because one lacks the security of being loved; conflict because one wavers to and fro between a choice of values imposed on him as conditions for receiving love and values which he himself recognizes as good and reasonable; frustration because he cannot fulfill the love-winning conditions he tries to satisfy; and fear because he is afraid of people, afraid to love and afraid to be loved lest he be hurt, lest he be further rejected as a person.

However, God has put in every person's psychological makeup a self-healing capacity, a natural tendency toward balance and growth into maturity. Just as when one suffers a wound, blood cells rush forth to form a healing scar tissue; just as when fever arises to destroy a deadly virus; and just as sweat pours out to protect the body from this burning fever, so likewise in the psychological order, there are self-healing, balance-restoring, pain-removing devices, which are often referred to as defense mechanisms. They rush forth to alleviate or cure these anxieties, frustrations, fears, and conflicts. But sometimes a germ-killing fever affects the brain and a cooling sweat causes dehydration; so too these defense mechanisms at times do more harm than good.

Joe, at this point — because he feels he has not been loved unconditionally and for his own sake — now feels miserable. Because he cannot love himself, cannot accept himself as he is in himself, he continues to strive to do, avoid, become, achieve or possess what he now feels as necessary to win love, acceptance, worth. In this state of soul, a number of defense mechanisms are developed. I will describe a variety of them and try to show how they stem from and are closely related to Joe's self-image and his lack of self-love.

PROJECTION

Joe looks at himself and sees not the sparkle of a glittering diamond but the ugly dark smudges of faults and weaknesses. Darkest of all are the ones which he feels keep him from winning the conditional love offered to him by his parents, teachers, and others. But the more he focuses his attention on these dark spots, the less loved he feels and the more he hates himself. So, what does he do? There arises in him a handy little defense mechanism called projection by which he covers these dark blots with a brightly colored curtain and projects them into other people. Finding fault with others is much easier and less painful.

People ask, "Why is Joe such a fault-finder? Is he that proud?" Maybe. But more than likely it is because he is insecure. He is criticizing himself in others because he does not love himself enough. He seems to be finding fault with others; but really it's an unconscious, less painful way of hating himself.

RATIONALIZATION

Another type of defense mechanism Joe acquires is that of rationalization. He finds that to admit faults, mistakes, sins, weaknesses is very painful because it tarnishes his self-image. A fault or two, even just tiny ones, have the same effect as pouring a bottle of black ink on a diamond. It makes him feel less loved and less lovable. He loves himself less. He hates himself. So, he pulls out a whitewash brush and gets to work.

People say, "Why isn't Joe more genuine and honest? Why does he lie and make so many excuses? Why doesn't he have respect for the truth?" Is it because he is proud? No. It is because he doesn't know that right or wrong, weak or powerful, perfect or imperfect, he is, as a person, loved and lovable. Well, actually he does know it. Joe is now in high school and has learned of his dignity and lovableness in books, sermons, and in the Gospels. But he never really experienced it, and he does not feel it. Deep down inside of himself something keeps telling him he is no good. Joe still hates himself. He has yet to meet the understanding heart who will love him as he is. Or maybe he has met many but communicated with none. He is walled up inside of himself, and as much as he craves for it, he refuses to accept love, is afraid of it. He doesn't believe that he can be loved.

SHYNESS

In fact, this inability to communicate becomes Joe's biggest difficulty. He cannot relate well to others. He cannot open himself even to a friend. He has no way of discovering whether there really are people who would accept and love him as he is, with no strings attached, no conditions. He will not dare to reveal to anyone his inner

thoughts and feelings, especially those dark spots, the smudges that hide the diamond. Why? Because another defense mechanism has taken over. We call it shyness — fear of people. He is bottled up in himself. He avoids people. His conversations are impersonal, lest his unlovable, hateful, inferior self be discovered and rejected. Baseball, science, the weather and such impersonal topics he finds safe. Public speaking, expressing his emotions, meeting strangers — these things he finds difficult. Even when alone and doing nothing he feels he is being attacked, criticized, and rejected.

Why is he so shy and self-conscious and sensitive? Is it true that, as some spiritual directors have told him, he has pride of timidity? Probably not. More than likely he just doesn't love himself enough. But in one way they are right. If basically humility is truth and pride is a lie, then for a man to deny that he is a beautiful diamond; to deny that he is loved and lovable and loved first by God would be the greatest lie and hence the greatest act of pride. But it is not our purpose here to judge Joe; for only God knows how much divine love Joe freely and knowingly resisted. What we are trying to do is to find out how Joe got the way he is and to find out the best way he can be helped.

Joe lacks initiative and creativity. To be different, to try something new he finds difficult and dangerous. Why? Because it involves risks and above all it invites criticism. And for him criticism or failure is too painful. For him it means more rejection as a person, a further smudging of the diamond.

SORRY FOR SELF
Another aspect of Joe's character is that he often feels sorry for himself. He has moods of depression in

which he keeps reminding himself how miserable he is. Here again the root cause is that Joe does not love himself enough. He paints such a miserable, pessimistic picture of himself that no one could help but feel sorry for him. Certainly Joe can't resist the urge. Self-pity makes him feel better.

ANGER

But his reaction to his self-image is not always one of bittersweet self-pity. He at times gets violently angry when he commits a fault, because he feels that this makes him appear even more corrupt and ugly. When this happens he sometimes punishes himself morbidly, or he will use projection to punish himself in others with anger, resentment, and even violence. It's easier that way. It's a more convenient and less painful way of hating and punishing himself – IN OTHERS.

Why is Joe a tiger? Why does he scream at people and lose his cool? Is it a lack of charity? On the surface it certainly seems to be. But perhaps the real cause is that he does not love himself. Our Lord did say "Love your neighbor AS YOURSELF."

LETTER OF LAW

Joe, in spite of his many faults, tends to observe rules, laws, and regulations of all sorts with mechanical precision. He tries to be meticulous about everything, and adheres to a rule of life with very little flexibility and deviation from the letter of the law. For him, laws and rules are more important than people. Laws give him security. People don't. From his early experiences in life he has found that perfect observance of rules and laws enables him to see himself as a diamond; enables him to regard himself as lovable; enables him to win love and recognition; gives him a feeling of self-worth; and above all, enables him to avoid the painful experience of seeing himself as less than perfect. For him to be seen as less than perfect is a major crisis. He doesn't love himself unconditionally enough to enjoy being imperfect, to glory with St. Paul in his infirmities.

LONELY

Perhaps Joe's most painful experiences are in his search for friendship. Insecure and starving for love, he is very lonely. In his protective shell, in his isolation he yearns for companionship; but because of the intensity of his craving for love he easily falls into excessive attachments. His love tends to become all-absorbing, exclusive, and jealous. Moreover, the intensity of his passionate craving for love and friendship has bodily reactions that can take the form of temptations against purity.

His spiritual guide tells him to avoid the occasion, mortify himself, pray more to the Blessed Virgin. Good advice, but does it reach the source? Or does it merely treat symptoms? Another confessor says that it is simply the work of the devil. Perhaps, but is Satan to blame for everything? Another confessor says that it is all the evil surging out of his corrupt inner being. But that idea was condemned with Calvinism and Jansenism. Maybe the real cause of his impurity is something very simple — the insecurity of not feeling loved. Maybe if Joe didn't feel such a neurotic craving for love, maybe if he were not so insecure, maybe if he felt himself loved and lovable . . . .

After a few agonizing experiences of this kind, Joe decides that it is safer and less painful not to have friends. He begins to realize that in his wishful thinking he has been idealizing people. He has been putting close friends on a pedestal and trying to capture them with a possessive love; but each time he finds himself frustrated and rejected because he has been loving a fantasy, a desert mirage. He does not know that love must be based on truth, on a mutual acceptance by two people of both the good and bad in each other. But how can he love another unconditionally when he does not yet know how to love himself? He decides that friendship is too dangerous. He withdraws from people into further isolation, becoming more impersonal than ever, and thus cuts off all hope of experiencing unconditional love, his only salvation.

CHAPTER III
MORE DEFENSE MECHANISMS

So far I have listed only a few of the many defense mechanisms connected with Joe's failure to love himself. I feel that the phrase "defense mechanism" is inadequate as a general term to cover all the faults, neuroses, sins, and bad habits that stem from this negative regard for self, from failure to love self. I prefer to distinguish two kinds of reactions: 1) defense mechanisms; 2) love-seeking mechanisms. For example, projection and shyness would be primarily defensive; whereas boasting and showing-off would be love-seeking. Perhaps it might be better to classify these reactions as: 1) hate-avoiding and rejection-avoiding; 2) love-seeking and acceptance-seeking. Exclusive, inordinate attachments to people would be of the love-seeking variety.

OVER-ACHIEVER

Because Joe feels, unconsciously, that he can win love and esteem, which he so craves, by accomplishing great things, he has a flare for bigness, extravagance, magnificence — anything that attracts attention and praise. Great deeds, colossal achievements are his goals in life. But these goals are often unrealistic, beyond his powers and abilities. He is an over-achiever. He is overly preoccupied with the idea of great success. He seems to be compensating for, filling in for something he feels he lacks. Is he a vainglorious operator? Maybe; but more likely he just doesn't love himself enough.

FANTASY

Likewise, Joe's extreme sensitivity to correction and criticism and even to innocent joking has caused him much misery. Because he feels that his self-worth and lovableness is dependent on what people say and think of him, he interprets the slightest criticism of what he says or does as a total rejection of himself as a person. He cannot distinguish between what he does and what he is; and he thinks that no one else can either. To be truly and genuinely himself in front of others with all his faults, mistakes, and weaknesses would be too painful. It would lead him to a deeper self-hatred and to a further conviction that others do not like him. One who does not love himself enough to be free of the opinions of others cannot be genuine. It hurts too much. So Joe puts on a mask before others, often plays a role, acts, pretends. To others he often is obviously phony, ungenuine; but in his own dream world he thinks that he is real. This defense mechanism (or love-seeking mechanism) is called fantasy.

IDENTIFICATION

At times, Joe in his dissatisfaction with being himself tries to imitate a person he admires, a person he would like to be. But he goes to bizarre extremes. In doing so, he becomes more phony, more ungenuine. He becomes two persons, or rather two half-persons; or to express the reality more exactly, he becomes less a person. He is rejecting the person that he really is and trying to substitute a person he is not. This mechanism is called identification. It sometimes leads people to believe they are Napoleon or a movie star, leads them to believe they have gifts and abilities which they do not possess.

AGREES WITH EVERYONE

An aspect of Joe's personality which, though tragic, can be rather humorous at times is his tendency toward agreement with almost everything people say to him. To him, in the very same conversation, black can be not only white, but also pink, purple, blue, and yellow. He wants to be on good terms with everyone, wants to be liked by everyone. It is his starving for love that makes him a perfectly acquiescing, forever agreeable "nice guy." To win approval and love, to protect himself against painful rejection, his life is one stream of "Yes, indeed." "Why, of course!" "You were never so right." Needless to say, Joe is a "nice guy" to have around. But how genuine is he? Is he a person?

Here again Joe is to a large extent the victim of conditional love. Coupled with his failure to receive unconditional love was an experience of strictness and domination on the part of his parents. Whenever he dared to disagree with his parents or think for himself, he experienced painful rejection. To win his parents' love and to avoid their anger and punishments, which he rightly or wrongly interpreted as a total rejection of himself, he adopted as a way of life the slogan "Always be agreeable. Live and let live."

SUSPICIOUS

Because Joe sees himself as bad, corrupt, and unlovable, he is very suspicious and distrustful of himself. And this self-distrust, which is one of the forms self-hatred takes, he projects into others and he tends to trust no one. He is very suspicious of people in general.

HYPOCHONDRIAC

Moreover, Joe tends to be a hypochondriac. He considers the attention and loving tender care he receives when ill as well worth the physical pain he induces into his body. At times, the illness is just another way of defending himself from some obligation he fears or failed to fulfill. Again, these phenomena can be traced to a lack of self-love.

FEAR

Perhaps the predominant feeling in Joe is that of fear. He is afraid to love, afraid to be loved. He is afraid of rejection. Out of fear, his mind is closed to much of his experience. He has many blind spots. He shies away from new things, is afraid to venture into the "unsafe" unknown. So he lives in a rut, in a set pattern of thinking and acting. He is not open to reality. Insecurity saturates and colors his whole life. "Perfect love drives out fear" (I John 4:18). But Joe has yet to experience this perfect love, which I will call UNCONDITIONAL LOVE.

Adrian Van Kaam in his book, *Religion and Personality,* seems to be describing Joe in the following quotation:

> If we did not feel accepted for what we were at home, we are always somewhat afraid that God and the people around us may reject us, dislike us, or condemn us.

> We are constantly on guard, watching ourselves so that we may not think, feel, or say something imperfect which may bring upon us the rejection and dislike that we anticipate because of our unfortunate experiences as children.

Likewise the following quotation from a letter written to Carl Rogers and quoted in his article, "The Interpersonal Relationship," describes Joe's background:

I am beginning to feel that the key to the human being is the attitude with which the parents have regarded him. If the child was lucky enough to have had parents who have felt proud of him, wanted him just as he was, this child grows into adulthood with self-confidence, self-esteem . . .

But there are parents who would like their children if they were changed, altered, different; if they were smarter, if they were better. Always, if, if, if. The offspring of these parents have trouble because they never had the feeling of acceptance. These parents don't really like their children.

They would like them if they were like someone else. Basically the parent seems to feel: 'I don't like *this* child, this child before me.' They don't say that. But I am beginning to believe that it would be better for all concerned if they did. It wouldn't leave such horrible ravages on these unaccepted children.

PARENTS

With regard to the parental influence in the personality development of persons such as Joe, it could well be that they are not at fault in giving the impression that the love they give their children is conditional. It might be that they are imposing an outdated European cultural pattern on American children. It could be that their whole outlook on life and love is tinged by Jansenism or Calvinism, by a belief that emotions are evil, that the body is evil. Their faulty approach may be due to ignorance of child-rearing principles. Or it may be that they themselves are insecure and fail to love themselves — because of the training they themselves had received from their parents. They are simply doing to others what was done to themselves.

Certainly the influence of one's parents is not to be underestimated. To a child parents symbolize all of humanity. As a result, a child all during his life will unconsciously tend to react to others the same way he reacted to his parents and other members of his family in early childhood. Likewise, he will tend to feel that others — the whole world — judge, evaluate, love or hate him as his parents did.

INSECURITY

This feeling of being unloved may be a result of a compulsive desire for money, status and luxuries, or it may be caused by a miserly stinginess about these things. If these are regarded by parents as criteria of worth and success in life, then they can be another symptom of love-starving insecurity.

One's own body image, too, can play an important role in personality development. Although we cannot truly judge the beauty of the human person from the outward appearance of the body, yet many people do. The natural beauty of a person exceeds all the natural beauty to be found in the universe. It's the Creator's masterpiece. Yet many people feel judged and evaluated by the shape, form, height or lack of height of their bodies. With Joe, it's his general, overall ugliness which adds to his feeling of rejection. He feels as Rudolph, the Red-nosed Reindeer, felt prior to that foggy Christmas night, and spends his life trying to win the fame and glory of Rudolph through great and heroic deeds.

REPRESSION

Another defense mechanism, the most harmful of all, is called repression. It is a device by which one denies the reality of what he experiences. He not only denies it. He shoves it deep into a dark closet of his soul called the "unconscious," slams the door shut, locks it, and throws the key away. It serves its purpose in driving out of consciousness painfully unpleasant memories and experiences; but it is extremely harmful in that it hides the original experiences that led Joe to believe himself rejected and unloved and hence bad and unlovable. It conceals the reasons why defense mechanisms arose in the first place. It constantly stands guard lest someone open that door. It makes Joe avoid books, people, conversations, and anything else that would lead to door-opening self-knowledge. However, from that dark closet of the unconscious, these hidden, painful experiences continue to influence Joe's actions. Moreover, he continues to repress new experiences and truths which he interprets as threats — rejections of himself as a person. Repression takes away the pain of feeling rejected and unloved. He is not open to reality.

People then ask, "Why does Joe have blind spots?" "Why can't he see what is obvious to everyone else?" "How can he say that black is white?" The answer lies in that dark closet where his experiences of conditional love and rejection are imprisoned. That is where Joe can uncover the fact and the reasons why he does not love himself.

How can he open that closet?

CHAPTER IV
JOE'S PROBLEM

Needless to say, Joe is in a very miserable state. And perhaps the reader too feels depressed just considering him. But this unpleasant description of Joe's character is necessary as background for the beautiful and optimistic insights into human nature and divine grace which we will discover as we travel along with Joe in his odyssey toward becoming a person, a more loving child of God. For both Joe and the reader, it is the cross before the resurrection, the thorns surrounding the roses.

JOE'S LIFE TILL NOW

To help the reader understand more fully how Joe finally does rise above his inadequacies and weaknesses, here is a brief summary of his story up to this point.

1) Joe was born a beautiful gem (a diamond) of God's creative love. However, he does not know it.

2) He gets to know and evaluate himself (and hence to love or hate himself) by seeing himself in the reflection of the mirror of reactions which other people have toward him — especially his parents.

3) To the extent that others prize, value, accept and love him unconditionally, as he is in himself, with no strings attached, he correspondingly sees himself as intrinsically and unconditionally good, precious, of great value and lovable. And he sparkles with the love that he receives and reflects.

4) However, if he perceives that the love given him is only conditional; that it is inconsistent and changeable,

that it is turned on and off to reward or punish; that it makes demands and sets conditions; that it is based not on what the one loved is, but on what he does, accomplishes, avoids, possesses, or looks like, then he feels that his dignity, worth and lovableness must be earned and won. To gain worth and love he must satisfy the demands of others, must first live up to their expectations. He feels that his value and lovability as a person depend upon the opinion of others. He believes that he begins to sparkle as a diamond only when others recognize, appreciate, and praise his external qualities, possessions and accomplishments. He sees his value as a person to be something external to himself, something outside of himself.

5) Because he fails to fulfill the conditions demanded as the price for gaining love, he feels conflict, fear, frustration, anxiety, and he sees himself not as a diamond but as a hateful object.

6) To alleviate this pain and to win love, he develops defense mechanisms. He stops being himself. He tries to refashion himself into an image — a love-winning image.

LACK OF SELF-LOVE

This detailed description of Joe's character shows that his faults have an underlying basic unity, and that they are all interrelated by a common cause which can be described as a lack of self-love. The faults, the defenses, are not to be considered as isolated ailments. On the contrary, they are symptoms. The disease is self-hatred — an underselling, a person-destroying, love-strangling evaluation of self.

However, Joe doesn't yet know this. It is hidden deep in his unconscious. He still keeps saying, "My trouble is that I love myself *too much.*" Unfortunately, his confessor agrees with him and tells him to humiliate himself, to meditate on his "sinfulness." Moreover, his confessor takes Joe's faults one by one, works on them and gives a fine blueprint for correction. He tells Joe, "Root out one fault a year, Joe, and before you know it you will be a saint." How far this is from the truth!

The following lines written by Erich Fromm in "The Art of Loving " give some idea of why Joe feels the way he does:

> "To be loved because of one's merit, because one deserves it, always leaves doubt; maybe I did not please the person whom I want to love me, maybe this, or that — there is always a fear that love could disappear. Furthermore, 'deserved' love easily leaves a bitter feeling that one is not loved for oneself, that one is loved only because one pleases, that one is, in the last analysis, not loved at all but used."

Although Joe is very dissatisfied with himself and suffering intensely, nevertheless, the spiritual progress he has made enables him to see great value in all his crosses. He sees grace in every mood, every struggle. He well knows that Our Lord's agony in the garden — where He underwent every form of suffering from fear, to anxiety, to conflict, to loneliness — has made holy and meritorious every possible condition of the human person.

SEARCH FOR HELP

But he feels that simply to accept things as they are is not enough. God has put in him a strong desire to rise above his inadequacies. It is in his very nature. Moreover, he can't go on much longer. He has nearly reached the breaking point. He doesn't know it; but he is looking with

Christ for the angel who is to come to Gethsemane. But where is he? That is the real problem. Joe is walled up inside himself, isolated from deep interpersonal relationships. What little effort he occasionally made to open up, to reveal his heart to a friend, to a spiritual director was in vain. He was always disappointed. They belittled his problems; criticized him; told him he was making a mountain out of a molehill; cut him off; babied him; gave him advice and detailed blueprints. They did everything but listen to him, everything but understand him and take him as he was.

So, after years of lonely isolation, his faults, his defenses become more and more ingrained. He finds it more and more difficult to maintain the false image he has created of himself. His faults begin to bubble to the surface as his image-creating defenses break down. As time goes by his unconscious self-hatred becomes more and more conscious; but he does not yet see the connection between his self-hatred and his problems.

In his frustration, Joe says to himself, "If only I could start all over again, be born again. If only I could start afresh in an atmosphere that is different." And Joe is closer than he realizes; for Our Lord once said, "Unless you turn and become as little children . . . . "

We shall see.

CHAPTER V
AN UNDERSTANDING HEART

When Joe's self-disgust and self-hatred reaches a degree he finds unbearable, he decides he must get help. But to whom can he go? "Who would understand me?" he asks. "Who wouldn't laugh at me?" In desperation, he finally chooses another spiritual guide, one who has a reputation for having an understanding heart. He decides to be open, if possible, to lay his cards on the table and face the consequences.

But he is afraid and very cautious. He edges in slowly, sending out feelers to see if Father will attack him and put him on the defensive as all others have done. He starts out in a general way, saying, "I feel miserable, ready to give up. I'm a mess, a basket case." Joe goes on to describe his feelings, his faults. Little by little he tests Father for negative reactions.

What surprises and delights Joe is that this Understanding Heart does not judge, or reprimand; does not console, does not analyze, does not disagree; nor does he even agree with what Joe says. He does not diagnose Joe's troubles and provide easy solutions as others have done. What Father does do is communicate to Joe an atmosphere of understanding, trust, freedom and unconditional acceptance. Of *understanding* because Joe feels that this person knows and appreciates his deepest feelings; of *trust* because this understanding heart has an optimistic view of man's ability to work things out for himself, think for himself and grow from within; of *freedom* because he enables Joe to speak freely and to freely be himself; of *unconditional acceptance* because he does not reject, threaten, attack, nor apply pressure of any kind. He does not analyze or manipulate. He prizes Joe in a warm and positive way. He is not even trying to *change* Joe. He accepts him simply as he is – unconditionally. In this atmosphere Joe feels free to share the burden he is unable to carry alone. He finds himself revealing to Father things that he was never able to tell to anyone before, not even to himself.

In this atmosphere of empathy, patience, warm understanding and total acceptance as a person, Joe – like a wilting flower just taken out of a dark stuffy cellar, given water and placed in fresh air and sunshine – begins little by little to be himself, perhaps for the first time in his life. He blossoms forth. He begins, in this atmosphere, to gain new insights into himself, begins to integrate his life, begins to be free.

LISTENER
Father is an intent, sensitive listener. He nods his head, repeats, rephrases and clarifies what Joe says and feels. He acts as a mirror reflecting Joe's thoughts and feelings. Often Joe has tried to figure things out alone, but he found himself in a fog – a fog of emotions. He was too close to himself to see himself. But now, through the reflection of himself in the kind eyes of this counselor, he can see himself and his problems more clearly, more realistically, more objectively. In so doing, he discovers that in many ways he has not been genuine. He admits to himself that he has been playing a role. He decides to drop the false fronts, or the masks, or the roles with which he has faced life. He is determined now to be himself – his genuine self.

JUST A FEATHER

In this safe and free atmosphere of warm understanding and unconditional positive regard Joe discovers how much of his life is determined by a desire to respond to the demands of others. He realizes that he is only trying to think and feel and behave in the way that others expect and demand of him, that he seems to have no self of his own. He says:

"Never in all my life have I been truly honest with myself. Actually, I don't even know my real self. I've been just playing a sort of false role. I was a slave to what others think. Why, I wasn't even a human person. I didn't even exist! I was just a feather."

This now is the moment we have been waiting for. Joe has made a leap forward in self-knowledge, the first step toward getting to love himself. And this was made possible because Joe can look at himself with freedom and safety. This is the "being born again." This is the "becoming a child." This is the redemptive second chance. This is the phenomenon that should be spelled out in bright, beautifully colored, 10-feet-high neon lights: Just as Joe's parents and many others in their conditional love have symbolized the whole of humanity, so too this understanding heart with his unconditional love symbolizes the whole human race. This is the reverse of his experience early in life. Joe is no longer a feather; he has become a diamond, a person. This is an incarnation of unconditional love, a second chance to be born again through love — a redemptive second chance to grow, mature and blossom in the fresh air and sunshine of a love that knows no conditions.

NO NEED FOR DEFENSE MECHANISMS

Joe finds that in this atmosphere his defense mechanisms have become meaningless and useless. It had never been safe for him to be himself; but now that he is not being attacked in any way whatsoever, he can lower his defenses. As for those love-seeking mechanisms that make him so phony, why bother? There it is — unconditional love completely free. It does not have to be swindled, earned, bought, demanded or captured. Now, Joe begins to grow — not through a systematic rooting out of faults but through love that makes him aware that his defense mechanisms, his faults are useless and self-destroying. He cannot completely root them out; for some are so ingrained that he must live with them all his life; but he continues to grow and learns to accept his faults and weaknesses. His love for himself becomes unconditional.

This love of an understanding heart is a loving first that sets people free. Joe too comes to *love himself first.* The rest follows. "Love is diffusive of itself." He does to others what was done to him. He too, in turn, becomes an understanding heart to others. Why? Because he now loves himself.

EVERY MAN

Who is "Joe"? He is every man and every woman. He is not just the great sinner or the emotionally troubled. Every man is a product of love or the lack of it. Every man is deeply influenced by both conditional love and unconditional love. Every man, at least to some degree, has a wide assortment of defense mechanisms. And every man, like Joe, regardless of his age, character and intelligence can "turn and become a child" and grow.

UNDERSTANDING HEARTS

Who is the understanding heart? First of all, He is Our Lord, the Heart of infinite understanding. He also is the non-directive counselor, provided that he is genuine, sincere, or congruent, as Carl Rogers puts it. And he is anyone, with or without counseling skills, who loves himself and his neighbors with understanding and unconditional love. Joe, through this encounter, becomes more and more open, becomes more deeply and personally involved with others. He develops many genuine friendships. Gone are the walls, the crocodile moat and the raised drawbridge that have been cutting him off from the only source of unconditional love, other persons, other diamonds.

PARABLE OF THE FEATHER

What has happened to Joe is clearly brought out in the "parable of the feather":

1) Joe is born a diamond.

2) He discovers who he is and what he is through interpersonal relationships — especially with his parents.

3) But his parents place conditions on their love for him. He cannot fulfill these conditions. Hence, he sees himself as bad, inferior, rejected and unlovable.

4) To win love and avoid rejection, and to alleviate the pain of frustration, fear, conflict, and anxiety, Joe sprouts many defense mechanisms. He has become a feather.

5) Defenses make Joe all the more miserable so he goes to an understanding heart and receives unconditional love.

6) In an atmosphere of understanding, freedom, trust and unconditional acceptance, Joe finds no need for defenses. He drops them, accepts love and begins to see himself as a sparkling diamond.

7) He begins to radiate to others the unconditional love that he himself has received. Because he accepts and loves himself, he accepts and loves others more and more.

8) And he himself becomes an understanding heart. A diamond once again, he now reflects in all its brilliance the Blessed Trinity residing within him.

POWER OF LOVE

There has been no discussion here about how the counselor created an atmosphere in which Joe could blossom and mature. Rather than explain counseling techniques, the purpose has been to show how an understanding heart can – with this unconditional love –create, inspire, heal and illuminate a person.

This power of love is by no means limited to counselors. Long before psychology began there were countless understanding hearts – the old grandma who can't read or write but listens with kindness and understanding; the bartender to whom many go with their troubles; the kind confessor who never read a psychology book.

ACCEPTANCE IS LOVE

Carl Rogers, in his book "On Becoming a Person," using psychological principles, arrives at what we would call a theological conclusion. Client-centered therapy stresses acceptance of self. Successful therapy replaces negative attitudes toward self with positive attitudes. With the gradual increase in self-acceptance comes a correlated increase in the acceptance of others. "The client not only accepts himself – a phrase which may carry the connotation of a grudging and reluctant acceptance of the inevitable – he actually comes to like himself. This is not a bragging or self-assertive liking; it is rather a quiet pleasure in being oneself."

Most counselors agree that the deepest need of people like Joe is to be accepted by the other person. Good counselors neither agree nor disagree with their clients. They make use of carefully chosen responses. They repeat, rephrase, nod and thus reflect the attitudes of their client so that he can see them objectively and piece them together.

This kind of counseling works, as Charles Curran in his "Counseling in Catholic Life and Education" writes:

"Because it stems from a true and Christian view of human nature: that man has a free will, that he basically is good and inclined to good.

"Because it removes defenses in order that man may have freedom to be himself, which is an important part of 'the freedom of the children of God.'

"Because it is based on understanding, which is the highest refinement of the virtue of charity."

CHAPTER VI
LOVE OF SELF

What then does it mean to love self? How do we go about it? The answer is simple: the same way in which we are expected to love others. Here too, it is Our Lord's words, "Love your neighbor as yourself," which supply the answer. Conversely, Christ is saying, "Love yourself as your neighbor." In other words, the same virtues we must practice with regard to our neighbor we must exercise toward ourselves – patience, kindness, gentleness, forgiveness, meekness. No one would object to a commandment which reads, "Thou shall not kill self"; but what about destroying self with self-hatred? What about maligning self, not forgiving self, being angry at oneself, holding grudges against self? Are these not sins against self-love? Is not attacking the person of one's self a form of mutilation or suicide?

When dealing with ourselves, we at times feel exempt from Our Lord's Law of Love. Consciously or unconsciously we tend to whitewash our brutal self-destroying thoughts and actions by calling them acts of humility. But humility is truth and the truth is that we are loved and lovable because God, by loving us first, made us so. Sometimes we call our self-hatred – after a sin – an expression of contrition. But true contrition is sorrow that we have rejected God's love and have thereby cut off the source from which we receive our power to love. What could be more contradictory than to try to express sorrow that we have not loved by making more acts of hatred – self-hatred?

THROUGH LOVE OF NEIGHBOR

In "Spirituality of the New Testament," W.K. Grossouw writes as follows:

"The precept of fraternal charity presupposes in the first place that the Christian love himself ('as yourself'). The implicit command for self-love is enjoined because we cannot really love our neighbor if we do not love ourselves. In what does this love of self really consist? First of all, in this: that we have squarely met ourselves and have come to know and appreciate ourselves. One must use here such an expression as 'to meet oneself squarely' since no one begins with a clean slate. To love myself means to learn how to limit and ground myself; to accept myself lovingly as a creature, and even as an image of God in my own limited but inimitable reality. It also means the accepting of my darker sides, my shadows, even the possibility of the evil which I did not do, but might have done as well as any other man, and in which I somehow have a mysterious share because of our common nature.

"Again this is not meant in the sense that true self-love precedes fraternal charity in the order of time. It is precisely through love of my neighbor that I discover myself and build up my own personality."

FORGIVE SELF

The supreme test of whether one loves himself is the way he reacts to himself after falling into sin. Joe, before beginning to accept and love himself unconditionally, used to experience long and painful moods of guilt after each fall into sin. This was true especially after sins of impurity or uncharitableness. He used to think that these moods were all feelings of sorrow for his sins; but now he knows that much of it is what psychologists call obsessive guilt feelings. He no longer lets himself feel low and miserable for hours or even days. Instead of hating himself and others, instead of punishing himself and others and thereby multiplying sins, he gently and lovingly forgives himself and uses the occasion to glorify God's compassionate, unconditional love by being open and receptive to it.

SUFFERING

Carl Rogers' theory of "Becoming a Person" raises a question about suffering and sacrifice. "Does maturing into a person rule out suffering to such a degree that a person becomes as relaxed as a sack of potatoes, carefree as a contented cow?" The answer lies in the experience of the many people whom understanding hearts such as Carl Rogers, Charles Curran and thousands of others have helped.

Let us again take Joe as a typical example. Long before he was cured, Joe had a deep appreciation of the value of suffering. He firmly believed that he was living Christ's passion, death and resurrection. Moreover, he was convinced that the Holy Spirit could and did inspire and sanctify him as he was in all his weaknesses. He knew that the Holy Spirit, with a flood of grace, permeated, elevated and used even his defense mechanisms to accomplish good works for the glory of God. He had enough faith to say with St. Paul, "When I am weak, then I am powerful."

OUTGOING LOVE

Joe knows that suffering is precious when united with that of Our Lord. He is certain that, with the grace of God, he will no longer suffer from the effects of hating himself, of defending himself. He is making an outgoing attempt to understand and love others. He wants his sufferings to stem not from turning in on himself and feeling miserable, but from patiently going out and relating to others – dying to self as a victim of love. Suffering and dying, yes; but not as a victim of self-hatred, self-disgust. He resolves that his Calvary will be in trying to accept others as they are. His motive in striving for maturity is to achieve a greater freedom in loving, a right to freely choose to love.

The end result is that he suffers more than ever. He finds that it hurts to put himself out enough to get involved with people. He finds that in trying to love unconditionally, he has to die every day, has to give up his privacy and desire for rest. Commitment to persons means that he must empty himself of his feelings in order to be able to feel with others, to sympathize with them; to enter into their world, to see and feel things from their point of view, to understand them. He finds that love involves risk. Daring to love those who hate in return is not an easy matter. Nor is it always easy to remain emotionally uninvolved. He has to love people enough to give them the freedom they need to grow from within. He has to be strong enough to take on the burdens of suffering people and not stagger under the load. This is the mission of an understanding heart.

CHAPTER VII
LOVE OF OTHERS

In exploring the unconditional love of an understanding heart, we have been describing what St. Thomas calls love of benevolence. We have in effect been fathoming the "breadth and length and height and depth" of the Sacred Heart of Jesus, the heart of infinite understanding.

Sad to say, it is often among religious people that "feathers" abound; and as a result there is no communication of love. Traces of Puritanism, Calvinism, and Jansenism are common. Such people tend to make God into a tyrant who loves conditionally instead of unconditionally as a loving Father. They tend to destroy the diamond. They destroy the person by viewing the body, the emotions, and human nature in general as basically corrupt.

Then there is the distorted American image of manliness, "I never say, 'Thank you.' It's a sign of weakness." Manliness is looked upon as personified by the cowboy who speaks with his guns — rough and tough on the outside but on the inside a big soft heart. Our Lord was a man "on the outside" too; He was gentle, kind, meek, and compassionate.

AS THEY ARE

In this world, the patience involved in taking our neighbors as they are is of supreme importance. In one of his letters to the Corinthians, the first thing St. Paul said about charity is that it is patient. St. Therese of Lisieux wrote: "True charity consists in bearing all my neighbor's defects, in not being surprised at mistakes, but in being edified at the smallest virtues." Patience is so important because the way we prove to our neighbor that we genuinely and sincerely accept him as he is and love him unconditionally is to bear with his shortcomings. Reaction to him in a negative way because of his faults or because of things we do not like in him is a sign of impatience.

St. Therese likewise knew that charity must be communicated. "Charity must not remain shut up in the heart . . . " Moreover, she intuitively realized that human weakness takes the malice out of very many actions that on the surface appear sinful and malicious.

It took Joe a long time to become aware of this. He used to be very pessimistic and see much evil, much malice in what people did. But now he realizes what defenses conditional love can arouse in people. His religious training taught him that passion, habit, fear, and violence can diminish or completely take away moral guilt; but never before now did he realize the extent to which unconscious defense mechanisms can influence a person's behavior. He finds it so much easier now to overlook the faults of his neighbors — even when their defenses are aimed at him personally. And this is possible because by better understanding and loving himself he can first accept himself and his own weaknesses. It was an understanding heart, Pope John XXIII, who said, "It is better to caress than to scratch."

LESS DEFENSIVE

Joe, having become less defensive, realizes that attacks upon, unfriendliness to, and criticism of himself are not really attacks but defenses or indications that people need love. As a result, he feels freer to wander into any group, to face any person however hostile, to mingle with sinners. That is what Christ did. Joe finds, as Schillebeeckx

He has everything.
He calls the stars
by name . . . for
He is their Creator

wrote in "Christ, the Sacrament of the Encounter with God " that "charity, a truly disinterested general love . . . disarms."

UNCONDITIONAL LOVE

It is very interesting to note that Carl Rogers – in discussing this helping relationship – finds that the need for positive unconditionality is perhaps the most difficult to prove. It is, likewise, curious to note that some criticize him for exaggerating the importance of this unconditional element of counseling. Others deny that it is even possible. Here in Korea, non-Christians often express puzzlement and disbelief in the face of stringless charity. Could it be that these psychologists are bordering on the infinite, on that which cannot be analyzed, only believed? Could it be that they are leaving their scientific field and touching upon a mystery – a mystery of God's unconditional love operating in man? I think so.

Let me explain what I mean.

Unlike human beings, when God loves it is not because He is attracted to something which He does not already possess. He has everything. He calls the stars by name. Everyone and everything He loves already belong to Him; for He is their Creator. Therefore, God's love is a giving, a creative love. Because God chose to glorify His love, He gave to man the freedom to become wicked, weak, little, wretched, and miserable. He wanted to show that His love goes beyond just creating and giving life. He wanted more than anything else to bring about the glorification of His love as merciful, compassionate, and redeeming. So He lifts up the weak, the little, the wretched, the sinful.

He sends His Son to show more clearly that His love is completely unconditional, by loving enemies, by loving sinners. That is the theme of love, the test of love in the New Law. Christ's love was and still is completely unconditional, since He loves us first and as we are. God's love is so unconditioned that He never stops loving anyone — even for an instant. When people sin, even if they fall into hell, it's not because God stopped loving them but because they refused to be open and receptive to His love.

In a way, the critics of Rogers are right. Among men there is no such thing as 100 per cent unconditional positive regard — only in God can it be found. But insofar as a person is able to love without conditions, to that extent he is sharing in God's unconditional love.

CHAPTER VIII
HOW TO LOVE OTHERS

From his own experience, Joe learned quite a bit about human nature. As a result of his encounters with understanding hearts, his attitude toward people changed very much. He had developed the habit of directly trying to change people, to mold them into what he thought they should be. He would attempt this by pointing out to them their faults, by "telling them off," by ridiculing them, by giving them advice and blueprints on how to be different. In more subtle ways too he tried to manipulate people by joking about their shortcomings, by making comparisons. He felt that he could change people simply by telling them what to do or what not to do. His approach was through their intellects, but we have seen that the real problems are feelings — feelings of fear, feelings of self-hatred, and feelings of not being loved.

NOT THROUGH THE INTELLECT
Here is what Carl Rogers, after 30 years of helping people, says of such methods:

"It is possible to explain a person to himself, to prescribe steps which should lead him forward, to train him in knowledge about a more satisfying way of life. But such methods, in my experience, are futile and inconsequential. The most they can accomplish is some temporary change, which soon disappears, leaving the individual more than ever convinced of his inadequacy."

What Joe discovered is that people, like himself, do not change through an intellectual approach but through a personal relationship of sincerity, understanding, and unconditional love. People usually know what is wrong with themselves — at least their external faults; in which case there is not much reason for telling them. If they don't know themselves, it usually is because they are too afraid, too defensive to face themselves. In this case, telling them off or even politely telling them their faults only makes them more defensive, more self-hateful.

SAFE ATMOSPHERE

Joe realizes that most of the faults in people are not isolated realities in themselves, but defense mechanisms, symptoms of deeper ailments, a lack of self-love. He knows that the cure for this basic ailment is simply to love people as they are, to create a safe atmosphere in which people will not feel the need to be defensive, to fight back, to make excuses, to shy away, to play a role. When people are with him he wants them to be able to be themselves. He wants them to know that he loves them as they are with both their good and bad points.

NOT A TECHNIQUE

In a practical way, how does Joe go about conveying this love to people? First of all, love is not a technique; it is a genuine art. His method, his instrument is his own self, his own person. Joe knows that his own faults originally sprang from his failure to receive unconditional love. On receiving that love he learns to accept himself as he is. And his whole life changes in accord with these two facts. He likewise discovers that when he begins to accept other people as they are, to love them as they are without directly trying to change them, they too begin to change spontaneously. That becomes Joe's approach to people — to accept them as they are and in so doing create an atmosphere of sincere love and understanding. Then, freed from the need to be defensive, they will in their own unique way, at the time and to the degree that they themselves choose, become more and more fully the beautiful diamonds, the beautiful persons that God has made them.

ACCEPT

The supreme principle involved is this: Once you really and truly accept a person as he is and communicate this acceptance to him he begins to change. This does not mean that Joe becomes 100 per cent permissive, that he may never advise, reprimand, punish, or discipline. If his is a position of authority, he will often have an obligation to do these things. But once Joe has communicated an atmosphere of understanding and unconditional love people can better accept his advice and reprimands, because they realize that in doing so he is not attacking or rejecting them as persons. They know that he still loves them without conditions.

PEOPLE ARE AFRAID

What Joe realizes very clearly is that people generally are sensitive and defensive, that they are afraid to be themselves, afraid of being disliked or rejected. He knows that poor suffering persons often interpret the slightest disagreement with their ideas, or the faintest criticism of their actions, or the slightest attempt in a direct way to change them as a complete rejection of themselves as persons. These are sure proofs that they are not liked as they are, positive evidence that love extended to them is conditional. They might know it is not so; but that's the way they feel. Being deeply aware of this, Joe tries to be very careful lest he arouse defenses in people – not because he fears them, but because these defenses set up barriers to love; and he does not want to hurt people. At times, he is tempted to exclaim to a person, "Can't you see what's wrong with you!!??" But he knows that people don't want to see because it is too threatening for them.

NEW JOE

Looking back at his life now, Joe sees that he is not the same person that he was 10 or 15 years ago. Yet, people who do not know the "new Joe" tend to evaluate him as they knew him many years ago – as a show-off, a neurotic, egotist, etc. He looks around at other feathers-turned-diamonds and sees that although they too have changed a lot, people refuse to recognize that they have grown immensely. Joe thereby begins to realize that it is very wrong to categorize persons, to classify them for all time. Why? Because once you do, you begin to react to them according to your arbitrary category. Joe now tries always to see persons as becoming, as changing, and above all as unique – really beyond classification.

UNDERSTAND THEM

A great source of peace for Joe is his deep realization that it is not necessary to change people directly or to judge them. His task is not to evaluate people but to understand them. He knows that interpreting or analyzing another's life is too big a responsibility for him – or anyone; nor is it possible. Everyone is unique. He rejects temptations to sit in judgment on people; for he realizes there is so much he is not able to know about unconscious motives working in them. He no longer feels an obligation to make a happy ending to every problem by solving them all himself.

In his positions of authority (parent, teacher, etc.), when people come to him for help, instead of focusing his attention on their problems (their symptoms) he concentrates on them as persons. His aim is to make it possible for forces of growth and integration in persons to freely operate. He says to himself, "This person is capable! Trust him! Fear and mistrust will hold him back!" His former tensions which came from the feeling that he must directly help everyone who comes to him now tend to vanish.

Joe is aware that for a person to really change in a deep and permanent way he must, as Our Lord says, turn and become more like a little child; and this, as we have seen in Joe's parable, is possible only by being born again into unconditional love, by becoming open and receptive to love.

Joe, by being kind, understanding, and respectful of the personal dignity of everyone he meets hopes to communicate this love — a love that is so genuine, appealing, and beautiful that even "a feather" cannot help but recognize it and be receptive to it. But, as he well knows, he must first love himself.

GRADUAL CHANGE

Some readers might feel that the change in Joe seems too sudden, that his parable has too happy an ending. But the change was very slow and gradual. Although his encounter with an understanding heart gave rise to sudden insights and changes of attitude toward himself and others, he still after many years has many faults. In fact, he keeps finding more. But he has grown, has made much progress, and can better live with his own faults and weaknesses, and with those of others. Though still inclined to be independent and exclusive, he better appreciates the need for community, for "togetherness," and for community worship. He knows that he grows best in deep personal relationships with other persons.

OPEN TO ALL

These deep personal relationships depend on a most important quality – receptivity or openness. Before Joe met the understanding heart, he was closed in on himself, cut off from people by his own defenses. He could not relate well to people. But once having received unconditional love, he began to trust love, to have faith in love, to develop a taste for it, to look for it and find it in others. He had only several short meetings with Father; but that was enough for a start. It unlocked that dark cellar door and let in fresh air and sunshine. To state it briefly, Joe became more open and receptive to love.

Now he finds that he himself tries to relate to others with understanding and unconditional love. Even with persons he previously disliked and avoided, he keeps multiplying the experience he had with the understanding heart. And thus he and his new-found friends continue to grow in self-love and fraternal love. It is the chain reaction of love. The understanding heart did not directly change Joe. He helped him to be more open and receptive to love, helped him to relate well with others. This then is how he "becomes a person" – by letting himself be loved. And he found that by loving other "feathers " and letting them love him they all grew into more sparkling and beautiful persons.

The spontaneous receptiveness of a little child to the love of his father and mother, and the need for a "feather" to turn and become like a receptive child in order to become a "diamond" is just as true in our relationship with our Father in heaven. Being open and receptive is the starting point of our spiritual lives, but we must continue to be open in order to reach holiness. God's greatest glory is the glorification of his compassionate love. And we can make this possible only by abandoning ourselves to His love, only by becoming so little that we don't mind letting God as a loving Father reach down, lift us up, and caress us with compassionate love.

St. Therese reminds us that faults and imperfections (and we can add defense mechanisms) do not rule out a life of pure love. It is our weak, miserable, little selves that give God occasions to manifest and glorify His compassionate love. That is what she, trying to be so receptive as to completely satisfy God's infinite desire to love, offered to God on the feast of the blessed Trinity, June 9, 1895. She wanted to become and remain completely open to God's love and his infinite desire to be loved.

CHAPTER IX
GRACE

The parable of Joe and the understanding heart gives us a fascinating insight on divine grace and how it works. Grace is love – or more precisely a relationship of love that exists between God and man. Grace, moreover, permeates and elevates human nature. It is not a superimposed structure. It acts in accordance with man's nature. For this reason, the more we know about interpersonal love relationships – what love does to people – the more we know about divine grace.

KINDS OF GRACE

Theology distinguishes grace into many different kinds: sanctifying, actual, healing, illuminating, efficacious, etc. But from examining what love does to people, as in the case of Joe and many like him, it appears that there is only one grace – unconditional love. There are various types of grace, but they are really only different manifestations of one and the same grace. They are distinguished by what they do, or by their effects. If grace is an understanding, freedom-giving, redeeming, trusting, unconditional love, then it is easy to see how it can be distinguished by its various effects.

GRACE IS LOVE

Before proceeding to reexamine love in the light of Joe's parable, let us examine what we know for certain about grace. Grace is love and God is love. The inner life of the Trinity is love. "God is love and he who abides in love abides in God and God in him." Grace is often defined as a "sharing in the life of God." This is equivalent to saying that grace is a sharing in God's love; for His life is love. Furthermore, we know from Scripture that God's love is by its very nature a redeeming, creating, merciful, compassionate, giving love.

In Christ's life, we see that this love is completely unconditional. He loves us first and as we are. This love was not dependent on what we did to Him nor on how we loved Him in return, nor on how we received Him or appreciated Him. Moreover, we see that Christ's love is understanding, trusting, non-possessive, and freedom-giving.

How much of this love can we see in the understanding heart who helped Joe? First of all, the unconditional love of this counselor, this understanding heart, is seen to be creative and life-giving. By a total giving of himself, by identification with Joe, he helped him to become a person, gave him new life, enabled him to discover his identity, to be born again and become a child through love. Isn't this what sanctifying grace does?

Notice too how similar to actual grace are the dynamics of this interpersonal relationship of unconditional love. The understanding heart — without any force or pressure, completely respecting the dignity, uniqueness, and freedom of Joe's person, simply by creating an atmosphere of unconditional love — enables him to grow and blossom, to freely activate the potentialities that God has put in him, to release hidden powers. Joe freely and spontaneously radiates the love he has received into acts of love and virtues of his own. This is where we find actual grace — love seen as a power which produces acts of love.

Another type of grace is called healing grace. That unconditional love has effected a healing in Joe is very evident in the collapsing of his defense mechanisms, and in the removal of painful anxiety, frustration, fear, conflict.

Also, we speak of illuminating grace. Here again is another facet of unconditional love. The understanding heart creates an atmosphere in which Joe is able to use his own God-given intellect in search of truth, beauty, and goodness; and this without feeding or forcing knowledge in an authoritarian way. He helps Joe grow from within. That ordinarily is how God inspires: from within through the medium of another person's love.

Peter Fransen in his "Apostolic Renewal in the Seminary" compares grace to the result of the sun's light passing through a prism.

"The white light of a sun passing through a prism at a correct angle produces the bright variety of the colors of the rainbow. All those different colors have their own brightness and particular luminosity, but remain all of them but one aspect of the same reality. So, too, do the various graces in our existence realize only one reality of grace, that God, one and triune, loves me and dwells in me."

The lyrics of the Cursillo song "De Colores" touch on the same point. They paint the beautiful and joyful colors of spring; the bright colors of birds and of a rainbow; the sounds of a rooster and hen, and especially the love of brothers one for another. Everything is seen as an expression of God's love, a color of God's love.

CHAPTER X
TRUE HUMILITY

From what we have learned about the devastating effects of self-hatred in Joe's life, our notion of true humility should be much more clear. This virtue should be based not on a lack of something, but on an abundance of God's love. To say that I am rotten of myself, that I am nothing of myself is true, but only as a supposition. Humility is truth and the truth is that no man ever did exist "of himself." No one ever did and no one ever will exist apart from God's love. The truth is that there never was a time when God did not love man. And because God loves us first He made every single one of us lovable. An habitual negative concentration on our so-called "nothingness" and "rottenness" is both psychologically unhealthy and theologically misleading.

The cure for pride is love, as we have seen in the removal of Joe's defense mechanisms. By experiencing love we are enabled to be free, to be honest, to take off our mask of pride, to act genuinely, to see and accept ourselves as we really are in ourselves and in relation to our fellow man.

STARTING POINT
Theoretically, love springs from humility as the foundation of our spiritual lives. But in practice the starting point is love – the experience of being loved first and unconditionally by God, who abides in the understanding

hearts of our parents, friends, and superiors; the experience of being prized by our loving Father in heaven and our loving Brother, Christ, whom we encounter in a very personal way in the sacraments; the experience of being loved as we are with all our accidental weaknesses of human nature.

All of us, to some extent, have suffered because of the weakness of those who by their conditional love have fostered in us a false concept of what we are. And as a result, we have yielded, consciously or unconsciously, to self-hatred. Consequently, we need an atmosphere of unconditional love in order to be really convinced of our lovableness and worth before God and man. We need it in order to gather enough courage and strength to climb the steep path of self-knowledge that leads us out of the valley of darkness and fear, and rids us of self-destroying defense mechanisms. We need unconditional love to climb the highest mountain where we can gaze at the beautiful sunrise of God's love, whose rays will illuminate us and make us sparkle with all the colors of a rainbow.

Then we will be able to look at ourselves and love ourselves. We will love ourselves because we will see that we are beautiful diamonds reflecting God who is Love. And we will look around and see other glimmering diamonds, millions of them. We will see ourselves in them, God in them. And the brilliance of God's love shining in all of us, further illuminating and reflecting each other, will turn other "feathers" into "diamonds" of God's love.

CONCLUSION

It is by turning and becoming children again, by opening up to God's love both directly and through understanding human hearts, by accepting and loving ourselves that we can once again be born – this time of the Holy Spirit. This is the spiritual childhood of the Gospels. It is letting ourselves become diamonds, BECOME PERSONS.

We accomplish this not through our own power, but by offering ourselves to INFINITE COMPASSIONATE LOVE. God's grace is His unconditional love, because God is love. But we will not receive the fullness of grace until we begin to love ourselves.

How to Develop a Better Self-Image
by Russell M. Abata, C.SS.R., S.T.D.

A beautiful "self-help" book that should lead to self-discover, self-control, and a greater acceptance of self, others, and God. The author discusses the person your *training* wants you to be, the person your *feelings* want you to be, and the person God *designed you to become.* Blends practical psychology with a Christian view of life. Written by a priest-counselor. *$4.95*

How to Deal With Difficult People
by Andrew Costello, C.SS.R.

With common sense, sharpened by modern psychology, the author attacks a problem everyone has encountered. He discusses different personality types, communication, expectation, and ways to look "below the surface" to improve personal relationships. He integrates all this into a CHRISTIAN view and shows how God-centered vision should guide all relationships. *$4.95*